Wildlife
in Danger

Jen Green

Chrysalis Education

Distributed in the United States by
Smart Apple Media
1980 Lookout Drive
North Mankato, MN 56003

Copyright © Chrysalis Books PLC 2003

ISBN 1-59389-117-2

The Library of Congress control number 2003105011

Editorial Manager: Joyce Bentley
Picture Researcher: Terry Forshaw
Produced by Tall Tree Ltd
Designer: Ed Simkins
Editor: Kate Phelps
Consultant: Michael Rand

Printed in Hong Kong

Some of the more unfamiliar words used in this book
are explained in the glossary on page 31.

Photo Credits:
Front Cover (main), John Cancalosi/Still Pictures; front cover
(clockwise from top left), Klein Hubert/Still Pictures; Sabine
Vielmo/Still Pictures; Klein Hubert/Still Pictures; Mark
Edwards/Still Pictures; 1, John Cancalosi/Still Pictures; 2, Klein
Hubert/Still Pictures; 4, WWF/Australian Info Service/Still
Pictures; 5(t), Klein Hubert/Still Pictures; 5(b), John
Sibbick/Chrysalis Images; 6, Pete Oxford/RSPCA
Photolibrary/Wild Images; 7(b), Mark Edwards/Still Pictures; 8,
Mark Hamblin/RSPCA Photolibrary; 9(t), Galen Rowell/Corbis;
9(b), Vince Streano/Corbis; 10, Roger Garwood and Trish
Ainslie/Corbis; 11(t), Robert Henno/Still Pictures; 11(b), P.
Breson/Sunset/FLPA; 12, John Cancalosi/Still Pictures; 13(t),
Vincent Dedet/Still Pictures; 13(b), Peter Cairns/Ecoscene; 14,
Galen Rowel/Corbis; 15(t), Alan Barnes/RSPCA
Photolibrary/Wild Images; 15(b), David Hosking/FLPA; 16,
Hulton Archive; 17(t), Mike Lane/ RSPCA Photolibrary; 17(b),
RSPCA Photolibrary; 18, E A Janes/ RSPCA Photolibrary;
19(t), Mark Hamblin/ RSPCA Photolibrary; 19(b), Geoff
Moon/FLPA; 20, Mark Edwards/Still Pictures; 21(t), Farrell
Graham/Corbis; 21(b), Terry Andrewartha/FLPA; 22, Sabine
Vielmo/Still Pictures; 23(t),The Advertising Archive; 23(b),
Mark Hamblin/ RSPCA Photolibrary; 24, Ecoscene/John
Farmar; 25(t), Mark Newman/FLPA; 25(b), William S. Paton/
RSPCA Photolibrary; 26, Ecoscene/Karl Ammann; 27(t),
Ecoscene/John Wilkinson; 27(b), Klein Hubert/Still Pictures;
28(tr), Royalty Free/Corbis; 30, E A Janes/ RSPCA
Photolibrary; 31, Peter Oxford/ RSPCA Photolibrary/Wild
Images; back cover, Robert Henno/Still Pictures.

Contents

Nature at risk

The planet we live on is home to all kinds of wildlife. Experts have identified over 250,000 species (different types) of plants and well over a million different animals. This amazing variety of animals and plants is called biodiversity.

People depend on animals and plants for food, clothing, and medicine. In addition, plants supply the oxygen that animals need to breathe. You may be shocked to hear that many of the world's animals and plants are becoming extinct – that is, they are dying out completely. Even more shocking is that the extinction of many animals and plants is due to the activities of humans.

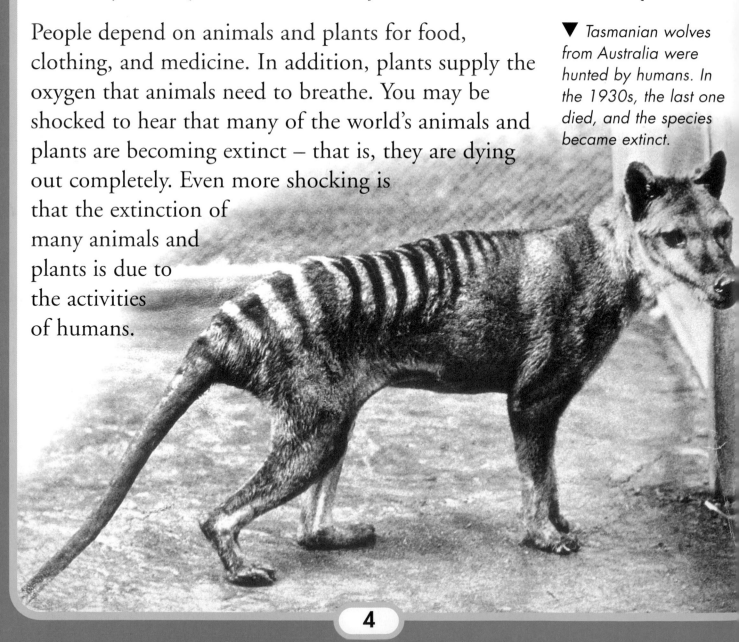

▼ *Tasmanian wolves from Australia were hunted by humans. In the 1930s, the last one died, and the species became extinct.*

In many different places, animals and plants are dying out because people are taking over wild lands and changing them to suit their own purposes. People are also hunting some creatures and killing others with pollution. On the bright side, many people are now working to save rare species and protect wild places. We can all help to save wildlife in danger.

◄ *The beautiful snow leopard is just one of the species that is now endangered (at risk of extinction).*

LOOK CLOSER

Extinction is a natural process. Throughout Earth's history, animals and plants have always died out, and sometimes many species have become extinct at once. About 65 million years ago, dinosaurs, such as this *Brachiosaurus*, and many other creatures, all died out suddenly. Now experts fear that people will cause a new wave of extinctions.

A natural balance

A habitat is a place where particular animals and plants live, such as a forest, swamp, or desert. Each type of animal and plant has features that help it to survive in its natural home. So, while creatures such as monkeys are at home in the rain forest, they could not live in the Arctic.

The animals and plants that live in a particular habitat all fit together to form a web of life. They are linked in food chains that maintain a natural balance. Plants make their own food using energy in sunlight. Animals called herbivores only eat plants, while carnivores only eat other animals.

▼ Penguins are suited to life on the continent of Antarctica. They could not survive in a rain forest or desert.

Over many years, living species very slowly adapt, or change, to become better suited to the habitat in which they live. This process is called evolution. If conditions change, species that aren't able to adapt quickly enough die out. Humans are bringing rapid changes to many habitats around the world, and many plants and animals cannot cope.

▲ *On the African plains, cheetahs hunt antelopes and antelopes feed on grasses. These three living things form a simple food chain.*

CLOSE TO HOME

Investigate the animals and plants that live in a wild place near you, such as a woodland. Identify the species you find using a book about local wildlife. What features help the animals you see to survive? For example, how do minibeasts escape from danger and how do they find food?

Destroying the wild

All over the world, people are threatening the survival of animals and plants by destroying the wild places in which they live. This is called habitat destruction. This destruction is happening for many different reasons.

▲ *Mule deer of the forests of North America are threatened by new towns, roads, and ski resorts.*

The world's population of humans is growing at an alarming rate. In just 200 years, the total number of people on Earth has risen from one billion to six billion. As the number of humans grows, so we take over more and more wild land to build farms, roads, villages, and new suburbs. Gradually, the small settlements and suburbs grow into major towns and cities.

CLOSE TO HOME

Many of us like to visit wild places, such as beaches and mountains, on vacation. We go to relax or enjoy sports such as swimming and skiing. However, hotels and holiday resorts can harm wild places. Too many visitors can disturb the local animals and plants.

▼ As cities such as Mission Viejo in the United States expand, they take up more and more wild land.

In many different areas, marshlands are being drained, forests cut down, and other wild lands tamed to make more space for humans. Most animals and plants are suited to conditions in a particular habitat. They cannot just move elsewhere. When all the wild land is taken, there is nowhere left to go.

Harmful industry

Wild places are being spoiled by mining for minerals and other natural resources. Areas of untouched countryside are also destroyed by factories and dams.

Parts of African grasslands, tropical rain forests, and other wild places are being ripped up to search for minerals and gems such as gold and diamonds. Fuels, such as coal and oil, are mined to provide energy for factories, vehicles, and homes. Drilling for oil is also destroying wild places from the icy wastes of the Arctic to the Arabian deserts. Mining is harming the oceans, too, and all the creatures that live there.

◀ Mining operations, such as this diamond mine, remove huge areas of rock and earth to gather tiny quantities of gemstones.

Wild lands are also disturbed when dams are built on rivers to generate electricity from fast-flowing water. The water builds up behind the dam to form an artificial lake called a reservoir. Plants are drowned, and animals are forced to flee from the flooded area. Recently, many huge dams have been built or planned around the world, such as the Three Gorges Dam in China.

◀ *Manatees are large mammals found in tropical seas and rivers. In South America, gold and tin mining are polluting the rivers in which manatees live.*

LOOK CLOSER

Animals, such as rabbits, are used by drug companies to check that drugs and medicines are safe for humans to use. Many people feel that this animal testing is necessary to save human lives. However, animals are also used to test products such as soaps, shampoos, and hairsprays. Do you think animals should be used to test these products?

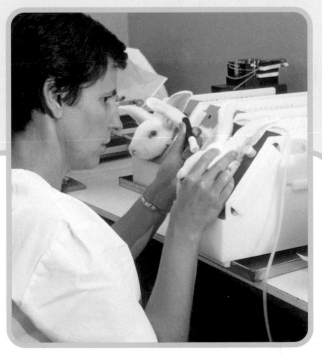

Farming takes over

Earth's natural resources include not only minerals in the ground but also the trees and plants growing in the soil. Wild habitats are being destroyed as forests are cut down for timber and wild grasslands are dug up to make way for crops.

Huge areas of the world's forests are being cut down for their valuable timber or cleared to make new farmland. The forests that are most threatened include tropical rain forests found near the Equator. These ancient forests are home to two-thirds of all the different animals and plants found on Earth.

▶ Pandas feed on bamboo plants in remote forests in China. Now these animals are in danger of extinction because the forests are being destroyed by people.

Vast areas of wild grasslands, such as the American prairies, have also been torn up to make fields to grow wheat, maize, and barley. In Europe, during centuries past, most fields were small and bordered by hedges that sheltered wildlife. Now most hedges have been ripped up to make large fields where machines, such as combine harvesters, can work more easily.

▼ *Just a few hundred years ago, the American prairies were a vast sea of grasses dotted with bison. Now the prairies have been replaced with farmland and few bison remain.*

LOOK CLOSER

As the human population grows in regions such as Africa, so more and more wild land is tamed to grow crops and raise goats and cattle. In hot, dry places, crops can quickly exhaust the soil of nutrients. Goats and cattle can strip the ground bare of grass. Then the soil dries up and blows away, causing land to become desert.

Hunting wildlife

Since the dawn of history, people have hunted animals on land and in seas and rivers. The meat was eaten, the skins used for clothing, and the bones made into tools. At first, simple weapons were used. Later, guns made the killing easier. Modern fishing methods have reduced the population of many fish.

Today, people in rich countries have no need to kill wild animals for meat because our food comes from farms. However, hunting still goes on in poor countries and in the name of sport. Animals, such as tigers and jaguars, are killed for their furs, which are used to make coats. The skins of crocodiles and other reptiles are made into shoes and belts.

▼ *Poachers kill elephants for their ivory tusks and leave the bodies to rot.*

Rhinos and elephants are killed for their horns and tusks, which are carved and sold as souvenirs. Killing these animals is now against the law in most countries, but the poachers still kill in secret. In tropical rain forests, colorful butterflies are caught, killed, and sold to collectors.

▲ Beautiful morpho butterflies are prized by collectors. So many have been killed that these insects are now rare.

CLOSE TO HOME

Fifty years ago, people used to steal birds' eggs to make egg collections. So many eggs were taken that some birds became rare. Now collecting eggs is against the law in most countries. People like these boys enjoy watching birds in parks and gardens but leave nesting birds alone.

Friends and foes

Some wild animals are now rare because people see them as pests or are frightened of them. Other animals are endangered because they are captured and sold as pets.

Lions, tigers, and sharks are just some of the animals that are killed by people because we see them as dangerous "people-eaters." Other hunting animals, such as wolves and foxes, are killed because they sometimes steal farm animals. Poisonous snakes and spiders are killed because they have a bite that is deadly to humans. Insects, such as locusts and beetles, are viewed as enemies because they damage crops.

▼ *This photo from 1930 shows European hunters with two lions they have shot. Today, it is usually against the law to kill these beasts for sport.*

◀ This caged parrot may have been captured from the wild. Ninety different species of parrot are now endangered because of the trade in pets.

Other animals are now scarce because people like them too much. Birds (such as parrots), reptiles (such as turtles), and even apes and monkeys are captured from the wild and sold as pets. Many die before they even reach the pet shop. Many others die in their new homes if they aren't looked after properly.

CLOSE TO HOME

Wild animals, such as monkeys, rare foxes, and even tiger cubs are sometimes captured to be photographed with tourists. These animals are often mistreated by their keepers who don't look after them properly. Think carefully before you have your photograph taken with a wild animal.

New arrivals

Some wild animals and plants are now threatened in their natural habitat because people have brought in new species that don't belong there. The newcomers upset the food chain and the balance of nature in their new home.

Cane toads of Central America help local farmers by eating beetles that harm sugar cane crops. In the 1930s, the toads were released in sugar cane plantations in Australia to control the beetles there, too. The large toads spread quickly. But instead of eating beetles, they hunted local frogs, reptiles, and small mammals until these animals became scarce.

▼ *The cane toad's poisonous skin protects it from enemies. In Australia, these toads are now a pest.*

During the nineteenth century, gray squirrels from North America were taken to Britain. They spread quickly to take over from their smaller relative, the red squirrel. Red squirrels became scarce. Gray squirrels, and also foxes and rats, now thrive in cities in Britain and other countries. They survive by stealing food left in garbage cans in streets and parks.

▲ Red squirrels once lived throughout Britain. They are now found mainly in the north and in only a few places in the south. Gray squirrels have taken over from red squirrels. Nobody is really sure why this has happened.

LOOK CLOSER

Wild creatures on islands are particularly at risk when new species arrive, because the existing creatures are often not used to being hunted. In New Zealand, a flightless parrot called the kakapo, shown right, became rare when rats and cats arrived. Previously, the birds had no enemies, but the newcomers killed them and also ate their eggs.

Polluting nature

Pollution is another major hazard threatening the survival of many thousands of living things worldwide. Factories, mines, farms, and towns release harmful chemicals that pollute the air, oceans, and land.

Chemicals sprayed onto farmers' fields to kill insect pests and weeds often harm other wildlife, such as birds and mammals. When the chemicals drain off into lakes and streams, they poison fish and other creatures. Eventually, these chemicals pollute the oceans. Factories, power stations, and cars give off fumes that form a weak acid in the air when they mix with water vapor. This then falls as acid rain, which kills animals and plants on land and in water.

▼ These trees in eastern Europe have been destroyed by acid rain.

Accidents at factories and mines can spread pollution over huge areas. In 1986, an accident at the nuclear power station at Chernobyl in Russia released a cloud of radioactive gas. The cloud spread far and wide. Lichen growing in the Arctic were poisoned and also the reindeer that fed on the lichen. People and millions of other animals were poisoned, too.

▲ *Thousands of Arctic reindeer like these had to be killed after they were poisoned by radioactive gas released during the Chernobyl disaster.*

LOOK CLOSER

Gases released by cars, factories, and power stations are trapping the Sun's heat in the air, which is making the weather warmer. This is called global warming. The warming threatens wildlife in many different habitats. Polar bears are an example of an animal threatened by global warming. If the warm weather melts the ice cap, then polar bears will lose their habitat.

Taking action

There is no doubt that hundreds of animals and plants are now dying out each year because of human activities. Fortunately, some help is at hand. Governments and wildlife organizations are now taking action to save wildlife. This is called conservation.

The most effective form of conservation is to save whole habitats rather than individual species. Parks and reserves have now been set up around the world to save local wildlife. In these areas, it is against the law to harm animals and plants. Wardens patrol the parks to protect rare creatures, such as elephants, tigers, and rhinos.

▼ Wardens in a wildlife park in East Africa carry guns to protect rare species, such as black rhinos, from poachers.

Wildlife organizations such as Greenpeace and the World Wildlife Fund (WWF) have launched campaigns to save rare species. In the 1980s, Greenpeace helped to put a stop to seal-hunting in the Arctic. Many governments have now signed an agreement banning the sale of rare animals and plants from their country.

▲ *This advert, made by the campaign group Lynx, convinced many people that it is wrong to kill wild animals for their fur.*

LOOK CLOSER

Yellowstone Park in the United States was the world's first national park. It was set up in 1872. The park protects 3,120 sq. miles of wilderness. Animals such as bears, moose, and elk (shown here) roam safely there.

Save our species

Animal and plant species are said to be endangered when only a few thousand, or even just a few hundred, are left. Wildlife experts take special steps to try and save species that are at risk of becoming extinct.

The first step to take is to find out as much about the rare animal or plant as possible. Animals that roam widely are sometimes fitted with radio collars so experts can track their movements. Rare animals are sometimes bred in zoos. The young may be released into the wild.

▼ *Eco-tourists on safari in Africa. Their money helps to pay for conservation in the wildlife parks.*

◀ This kangaroo is being fitted with a radio collar so scientists can learn more about its habits and movement. This will help protect kangaroos in the future.

LOOK CLOSER

Przewalski's horse is a wild horse from Mongolia in western China. In the twentieth century, these horses became extinct in the wild, but some survived in zoos. In the 1980s and 1990s, the captive horses were bred successfully. Now some young horses have been released back into the wild in Mongolia.

Zoos are not as popular as they used to be. Many people don't like to see animals kept in cramped cages. They prefer to see animals living naturally. Eco-tourism is a growing industry in many countries. This is when tourists pay to visit wildlife parks where animals roam freely. The tourists' money helps to pay for the upkeep of the parks.

How can we help?

Today, more and more people are realising that we should act as guardians for nature. There are many things that we can all do to help save wildlife and protect wild places, both at home and abroad.

You can help to protect rare species by joining a wildlife or conservation organization, such as the World Wildlife Fund or Greenpeace. Some organizations have schemes where you can sponsor (help support) your favorite animal. You could also organize a sponsored walk, swim, or cycle ride to raise money for conservation.

◀ *These souvenirs are made from ivory tusks, animal skins, and parts of rare animals. Never buy souvenirs made from rare animals or plants.*

Saving energy helps to reduce the pollution produced by mining and power stations. Save energy by switching off lights and other machines when they aren't being used. Using water carefully saves energy, too. Turn off the tap when brushing your teeth. Help to end the testing of soaps, shampoos, hairsprays, and similar products on animals by buying ones that haven't been tested on them.

▲ Take care of nature in your neighborhood by cleaning up litter. You could ask your teacher if your class can visit the local countryside to clean up, too.

▼ If your family buys a pet, such as a parrot, check that it has been bred from captive animals and not captured from the wild.

Litter harms wildlife. You can help to reduce litter by returning paper, glass, plastic, and other waste to recycling centers. Try not to use throw-away products, such as paper plates and plastic forks. Re-use plastic carrier bags when you go shopping.

Wildlife projects

Make a corner of your garden or school grounds into a mini-reserve for wild plants and animals. A well-stocked bird table will attract many hungry birds.

MAKE A WILDLIFE AREA

Here are some simple ideas for attracting wild animals and plants to your yard.

▲ Plants that attract insects can be sown in a window box if you have no yard. Never use slug pellets or weed killer in your mini-reserve!

1. Sow plants that attract bees and butterflies, such as buddleia, wallflowers, candytuft, and phlox, in a quiet corner. If you allow a small area to go wild, weeds such as nettles will attract butterflies.

2. A small pile of logs or rocks will shelter minibeasts, such as worms and sow bugs, and even porcupines and frogs.

3. Make a mini-pond by digging a hole and putting an old plastic bowl in it. Put stones and gravel on the bottom and stones around the edge.

BUILD A HANGING BIRD TABLE

Make this simple bird table, and leave stale bread, cheese, bacon rind, and nuts to feed the birds.

1. Make a bird table from a wooden board about 4in. x /in. Glue strips of wood along the edges to make a lip.

2. Ask an adult to drill a few holes in the board so water can drain away. The table will last longer if you varnish it.

▶ The bird table should be at least 4ft 3in. above the ground so cats can't reach it.

3. Attach hooks to the four corners, and tie strings to two of the hooks. Now loop the strings over a stout, overhanging branch, and tie the ends of the string to the remaining hooks.

CAMPAIGN GROUPS

World Wildlife Fund (WWF)
1250 Twenty-fourth St. N.W.,
P.O. Box 97180, Washington DC, 20090-7180
Website: www.wwf.org

Friends of the Earth
1025 Vermont Ave., N.W., Suite 300,
Washington DC, 20005
Website: www.foei.org

Greenpeace
702 H Street, N.W., Suite 300, Washington DC, 20001
Website: www.greenpeace.org

WILDLIFE WEBSITES

www.panda.org/kids

Animal Planet: www.animal.discovery.com

BBC's natural history website: www.bbc.co.uk/nature

National Geographic: www.nationalgeographic.com

www.kidsplanet.org

Rainforest Action Network: www.ran.org/kids_action

Rainforest diversity: www.forest.org

Wildlite facttile

- Sumatran rhinos of Southeast Asia are among the world's rarest large mammals. Only about 300 are left. These rhinos are hunted for their horns.

- Spix's macaw is a parrot that is now extinct in the wild. There are about 60 in captivity, and it is hoped that one day they can be reintroduced into the wild.

- Experts fear that up to 30 000 species of animals and plants may soon become extinct each year. At this rate, up to one-third of the world's wildlife could be lost in just 20 years.

- Rare plants are sometimes rescued from extinction by saving their seeds in seed banks. Kew Gardens in Britain holds the world's largest seed bank.

- Experts estimate that about ten percent of the world's trees are endangered. Of these, about one-quarter are protected in nature reserves or seed banks.

- Reserves and parks cover almost ten percent of Earth's dry land in total. The world's largest wildlife reserve is in northeast Greenland in the Arctic.

- An agreement called the Convention on International Trade in Endangered Species (CITES) outlaws trade in rare animals and plants. More than 150 countries have signed this pact.

- In the oceans, the great whales were hunted for their meat and fatty blubber for centuries. They were close to extinction when whaling was banned in 1986.

Glossary

Biodiversity
The variety of animals and plants.

Carnivore
A living thing that eats mostly meat.

Conservation
The protection of wildlife.

Eco-tourism
When tourists help pay for conservation in a natural habitat such as a wildlife park.

Endangered
At risk of extinction.

Equator
An imaginary line circling around Earth's widest point.

Evolution
The process by which animal and plant species very slowly change to suit conditions in their habitat.

Extinct
When an animal or plant species dies out completely, so that no more are left on Earth.

Global warming
Warming weather worldwide caused by the increase of gases in the air that traps the Sun's heat.

Habitat
A place where a particular group of animals and plants live, such as a desert or forest.

Habitat destruction
When a wild place where animals and plants live is destroyed, usually by people.

Herbivore
An animal that eats plants, but not animals.

Illegal
Something that is against the law.

Poacher
A hunter who kills animals that are protected by laws.

Radioactive
Giving out harmful rays. Nuclear power plants use radioactive chemicals.

Reservoir
An artificial lake.

Settlement
A place where people live, such as a village or town.

Species
A particular type of animal or plant.

Suburb
A built-up area, located on the edge of a town or city.

Index